BASS RECORDED VERSIONS

Sly & Family
the Stone
for Bass

Music transcriptions by Martin Shellard and Matt Scharfglass

Cover photo by Michael Ochs Archives/Getty Images

ISBN 978-1-4768-7147-9

HAL•LEONARD®
CORPORATION

7777 W. BLUEMOUND RD. P.O. BOX 13819 MILWAUKEE, WI 53213

Visit Hal Leonard Online at
www.halleonard.com

from *Fresh*

Babies Makin' Babies

Words and Music by Sylvester Stewart

Tune down 1/2 step:
(low to high) E♭-A♭-D♭-G♭

Intro

Moderately slow ♩ = 93

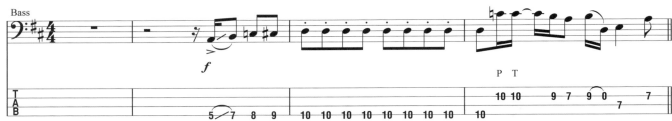

Chorus

Ba - bies mak - in' ba - bies, ___ oh, ba - bies mak - in' ba - bies. ___ Ooh,

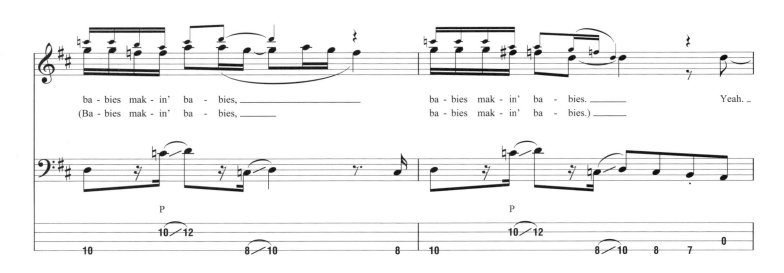

ba - bies mak - in' ba - bies, _____ ba - bies mak - in' ba - bies. _____ Yeah. _
(Ba - bies mak - in' ba - bies, _____ ba - bies mak - in' ba - bies.) _____

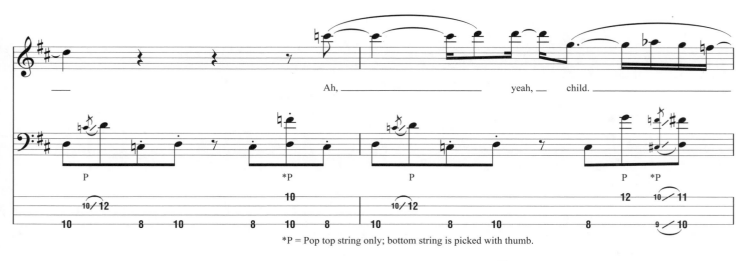

Ah, _____ yeah, _____ child. _____

*P = Pop top string only; bottom string is picked with thumb.

Verse
D7

1. From the womb _____ to _____

Voc. Fig. 1 .... **End Voc. Fig. 1**

(Ba - bies mak - in' ba - bies.) _____

Bass Fig. 1 .... **End Bass Fig. 1**

Bass: w/ Bass Fig. 1 (3 times)

_____ the tomb, _____ aw, ba - bies mak - in' ba - bies. _____ What you _____ say? _____

Bkgd. Voc.: w/ Voc. Fig. 1

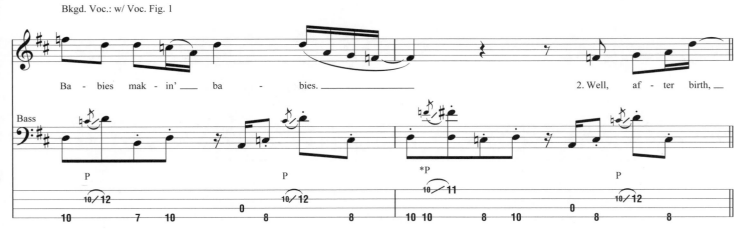

Ba - bies mak - in' _____ ba - bies. _____ 2. Well, af - ter birth, _____

Bass

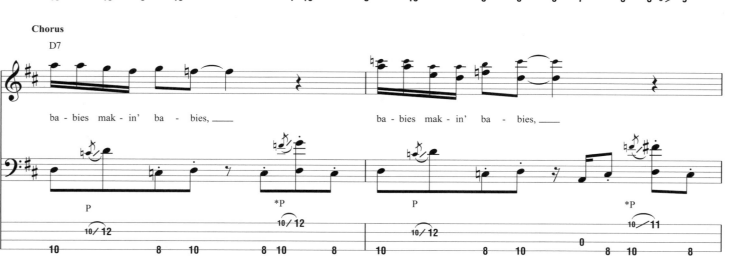

ba - bies mak - in' ba - bies, ah, _____ ba - bies mak - in' ba - bies. ___ Oh, ___

P   *P   P   P

*As before

Verse

Bkgd. Voc.: w/ Voc. Fig. 1

D7

whoa,   ha,   ho,   whoa, foo, __ hoo.   3. Two by twos, _____   pay - in'

P   P   *P   P   P   *P

Bass: w/ Bass Fig. 1 (9 times)

dues, _   whoa, wah. ___   ho, _____   whoa, ___ whoa, whoa. _____   What __ you say? _
(Ba - bies mak - in' ba - bies.) _____

Verse

Bkgd. Voc.: w/ Voc. Fig. 1

D7

3

Ba - bies mak - in' __ ba - bies. ___   Sing. _   4. More and more, __   ah - oo,

3

what the score?   Ah, ___ ba - bies mak - in' _____ lit - tle ba - bies. ___   Ha, _____

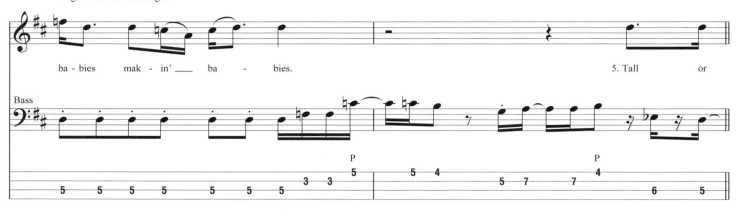

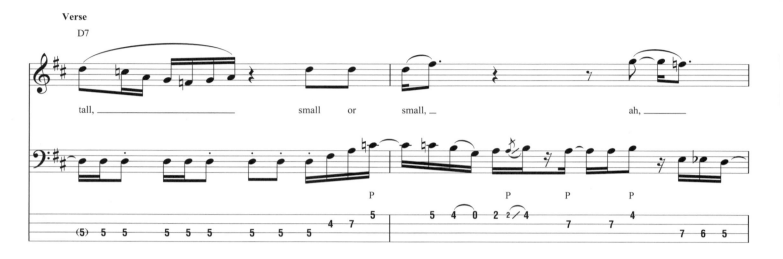

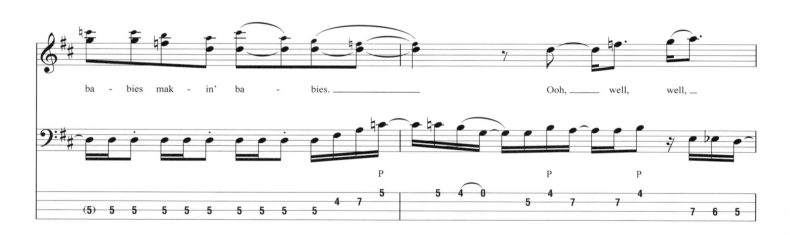

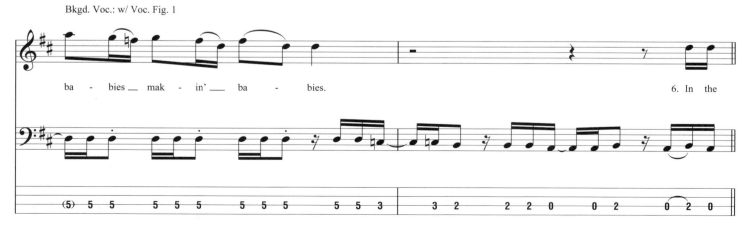

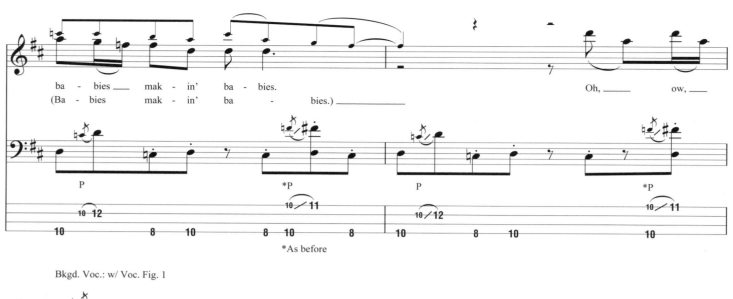

ba - bies __ mak - in' ba - bies.
(Ba - bies mak - in' ba - bies.) __

Oh, ____ ow, __

*As before

Bkgd. Voc.: w/ Voc. Fig. 1

ba - bies __ mak - in' ba - bies, ba - by.

8. Tell the

Verse
D7

truth, __ whoa, __ to the youth. _

Whoa, _ ba -

\- bies mak - in' ba - bies, _____
(Ba - bies mak - in' ba - bies.) _____

oh, ho, __ ho, ho. __

Dance to the Music

Words and Music by Sylvester Stewart

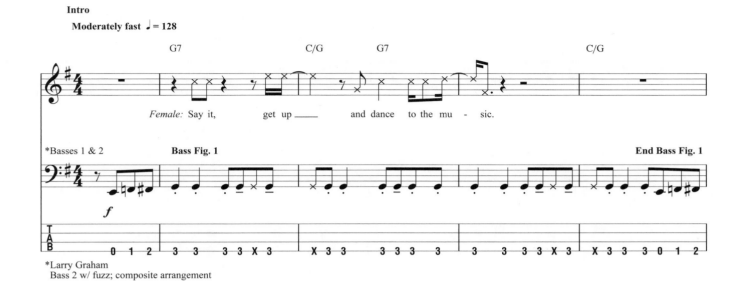

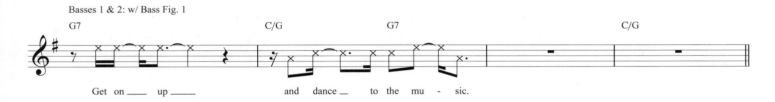

Pre-Chorus

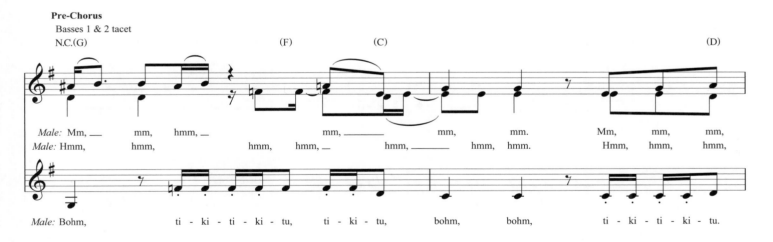

Chorus

Bass 2: w/ Bass Fill 1 (8 times)

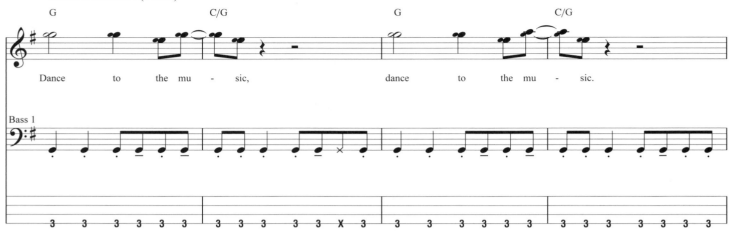

Dance to the mu - sic, dance to the mu - sic.

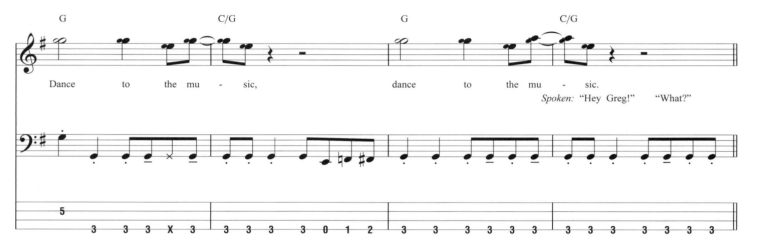

Dance to the mu - sic, dance to the mu - sic.

Spoken: "Hey Greg!" "What?"

Verse

Bass 2: w/ Bass Fill 1 (4 times)

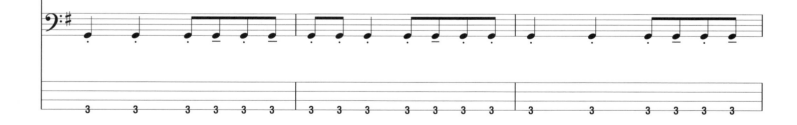

1. All we need ___ is a drum - mer for peo - ple who on - ly need a beat, ___

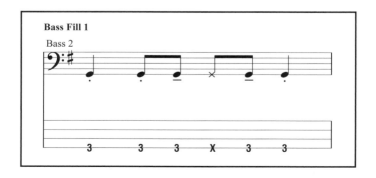

Bass Fill 1

Bass 2

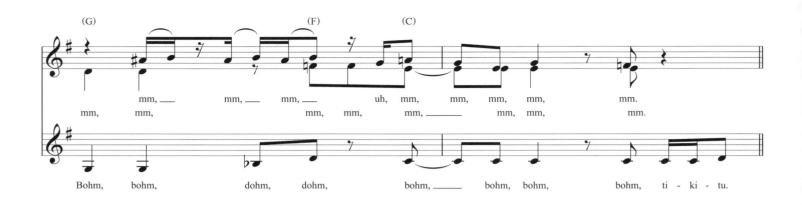

Outro-Chorus

Begin fade

Fade out

from *Stand!*

Everyday People

Words and Music by Sylvester Stewart

from *There's a Riot Goin' On*

Family Affair

Words and Music by Sylvester Stewart

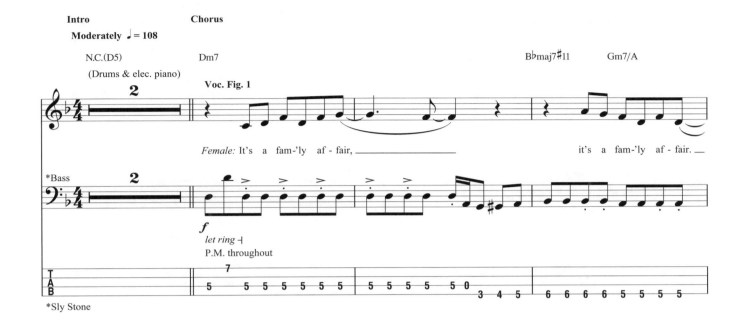

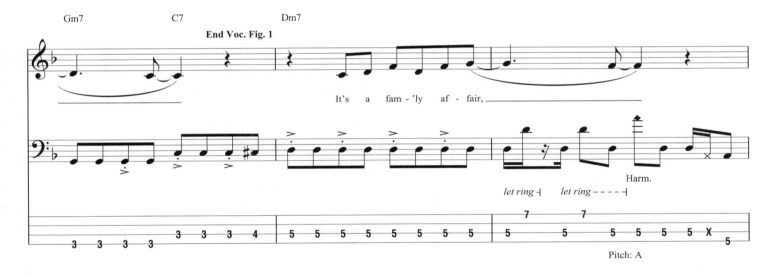

Outro

Doo, doo, doo, — whoa.

Ah, — ha, — ha, — hey.

Female: It's a fam - 'ly af - fair, —

it's a fam - 'ly af - fair. —

I Want to Take You Higher

Words and Music by Sylvester Stewart

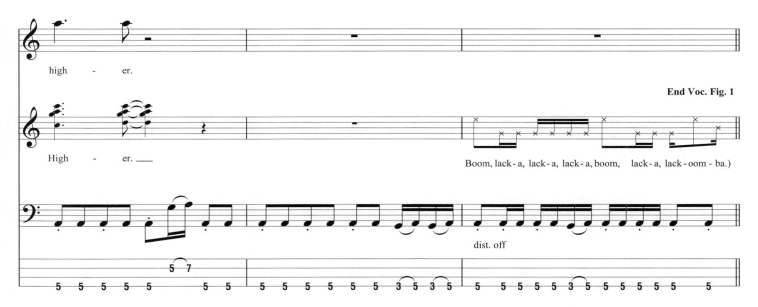

high - er? Ba - by, ba - by, ba - by, __ light my fi - re.

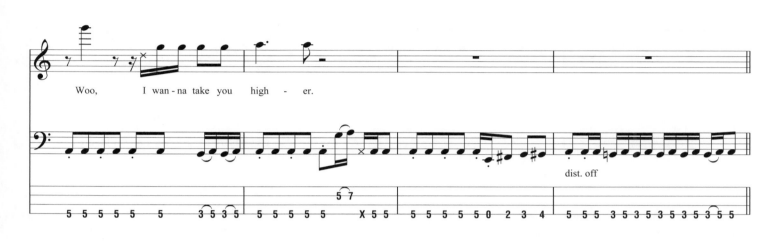

Woo, I wan - na take you high - er.

Interlude

A7(no3rd)

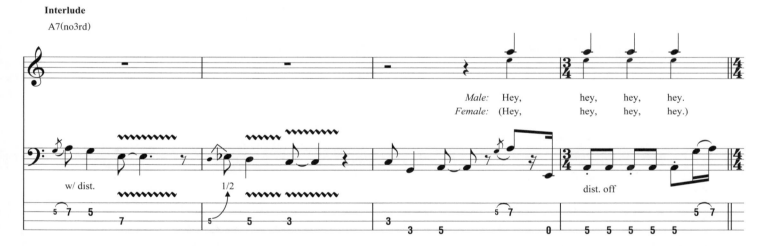

Male: Hey, hey, hey, hey.
Female: (Hey, hey, hey, hey.)

Harmonica Solo

A7(no3rd)

Voc. Fig. 2   End Voc. Fig. 2

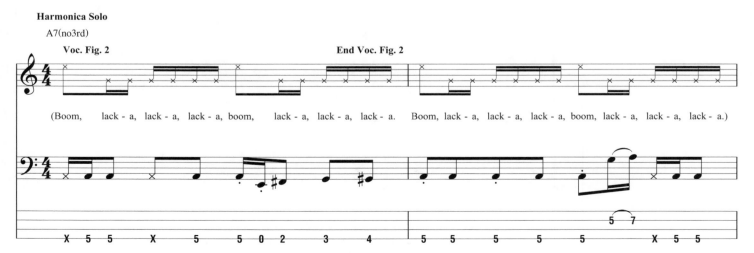

(Boom, lack - a, lack - a, lack - a, boom, lack - a, lack - a, lack - a. Boom, lack - a, lack - a, lack - a, boom, lack - a, lack - a, lack - a.)

Chorus

Bkgd. Voc.: w/ Voc. Fig. 3 (8 times)

A7(no3rd)

Bass Fig. 3

w/ dist.

End Bass Fig. 3

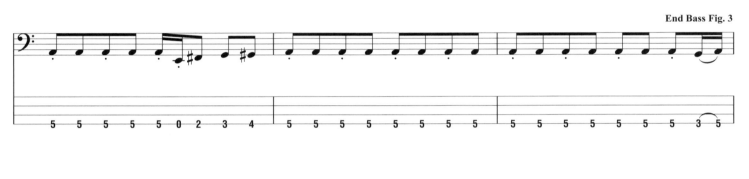

Won't-cha light my fi - re, woo, yeah, ha. Wan-na take you high -

Voc. Fig. 3

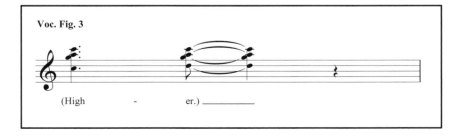

(High - er.)

Chorus

Bkgd. Voc.: w/ Voc. Fig. 3 (8 times)

A7(no3rd)

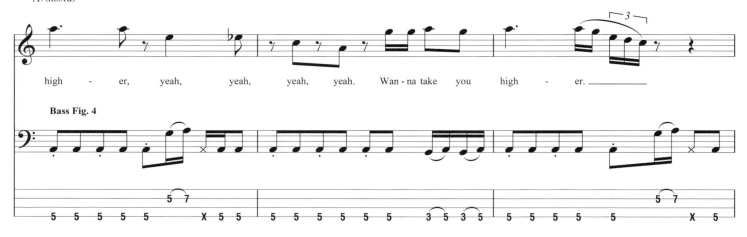

high - er, yeah, yeah, yeah, yeah. Wan-na take you high - er. _____

Bass Fig. 4

Ba - by, ba - by, ba - by, light my fi - re, ___ woo. I wan-na take you

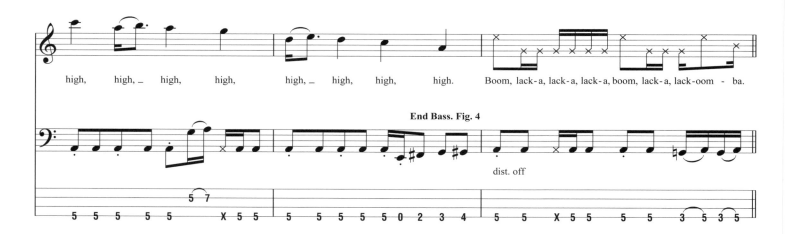

high, high, ___ high, high, high, ___ high, high, high. Boom, lack-a, lack-a, lack-a, boom, lack-a, lack-oom - ba.

End Bass. Fig. 4

dist. off

Guitar Solo

Bkgd. Voc.: w/ Voc. Fig. 2 (8 times)

A7(no3rd)

w/ dist.

Chorus

Bkgd. Voc.: w/ Voc. Fig. 3 (8 times)
Bass 1: w/ Bass Fig. 4

A7(no3rd)

Let's take you,   do you wan - na go,   with me, me,

and you, you?   Won't you light my   fi - re,   woo,   yeah.

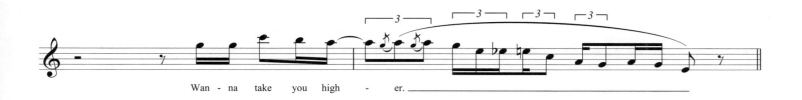

Wan - na take you high   -   er. _____

Trumpet Solo

Bkgd. Voc.: w/ Voc. Fig. 2 (8 times)

A7(no3rd)

Bass 1

Chorus

Bkgd. Voc.: w/ Voc. Fig. 3 (8 times)
Bass 1: w/ Bass Fig. 2

A7(no3rd)

Can you feel it?   Yeah. _____

Do you wan - na go high - er? _____ Woo,

Bass 1: w/ Bass Fill 1

ha.   I wan - na take you high - er,   yeah, ___ yeah.

Bass Solo

Bkgd. Voc.: w/ Voc. Fig. 2 (8 times)
Bass 1: w/ Bass Fig. 1

A7(no3rd)

Bass 2

Bass 1: w/ Bass Fig. 1 (last 2 meas.)

Bass 1: w/ Bass Fig. 1 (1st 2 meas.)

Chorus

Bkgd. Voc.: w/ Voc. Fig. 3 (8 times)
Bass 1: w/ Bass Fig. 3
Bass 2 tacet

A7(no3rd)

Hey,   ha.   I wan - na take you high -

Bass 1: w/ Bass Fig. 1

- er, _____ yeah. ____   I want to take you high - er.

Outro

Bkgd. Voc.: w/ Voc. Fig. 2 (till fade)

A7(no3rd)

Bass 1

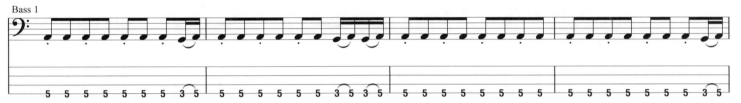

Ev -'ry - bod - y,

Begin fade   *Fade out*

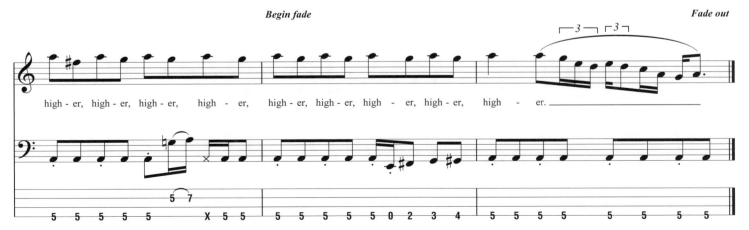

high - er, high - er, high - er,   high - er,   high - er, high - er, high - er, high - er,   high - er. _____

from *Fresh*

If You Want Me to Stay

Words and Music by Sylvester Stewart

*Tune up 1/2 step:
(low to high) E#-A#-D#-G#

Intro

Moderately ♩ = 101

A9(no3rd)

(Drum machine & elec. piano)

**Bass

*Originally recorded in standard tuning, the tape was sped up, raising the pitch 1/2 step.
**Rustee Allen

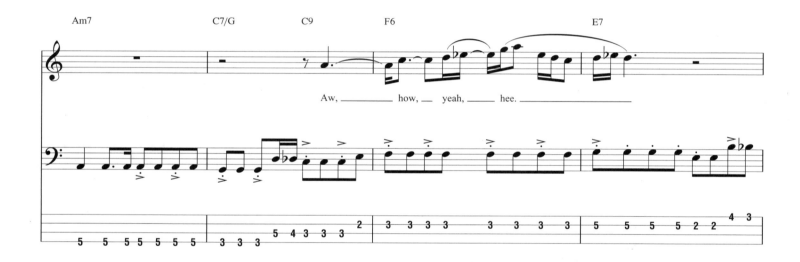

Aw, _____ how, ___ yeah, _____ hee. _____

Oo, _____ oo, hoo, ___ wow. _____   Yay, _ ah, _____ ha, ___ yeah. ___   1. If you

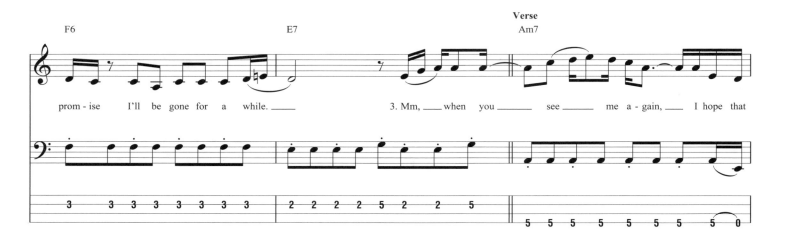

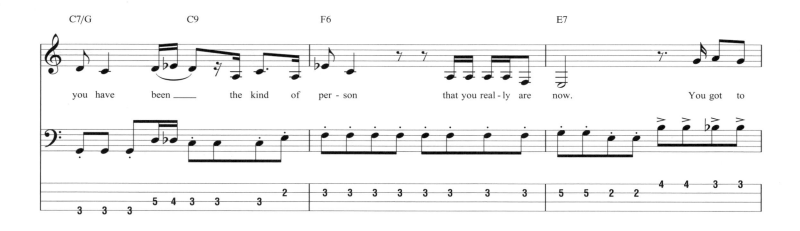

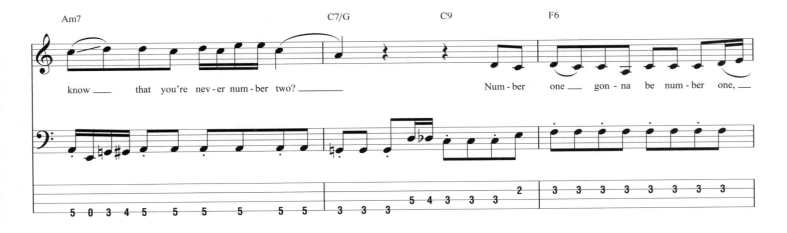

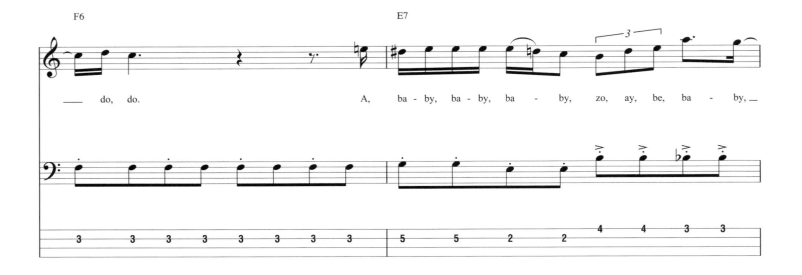

do, do.   A, ba - by, ba - by, ba - by, zo, ay, be, ba - by, —

— ba - by, ba - by, ba - by, babe.   I'm good — now.

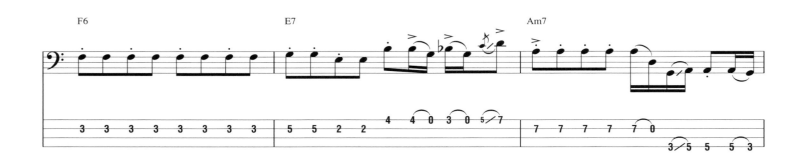

Begin fade

Fade out

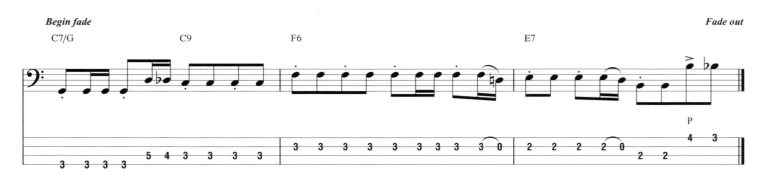

Life

Words and Music by Sylvester Stewart

Chorus

Bass 2: w/ Bass Fig. 1

_____ life, _____ clouds and clowns. _____

You don't have to come down. _____

Verse

Bass 2: w/ Bass Fig. 2 (2 times)

2. You might _ be scared of some - thin', look at Mis - ter Stew - art; he's the on - ly per -

- son he has _ to fear. _____ He'll on - ly let him - self get near. _

_____ He don't _ trust no - bod - y. If he _ stopped be -

in' so _ shad - y, he could have _ a nice young la - dy. _ Life, _

Chorus

Bass 2: w/ Bass Fig. 1

_____ life, _____ tell it like it is. _____

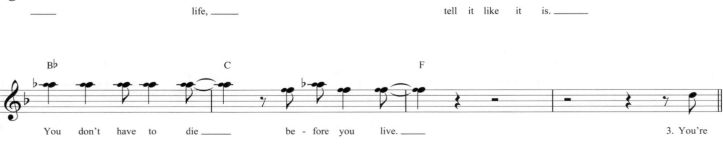

You don't have to die _____ be - fore you live. _____ 3. You're

from *Small Talk*

Loose Booty

Words and Music by Sylvester Stewart

*Tune up 1/2 step:
(low to high) E♯-A♯-D♯-G♯

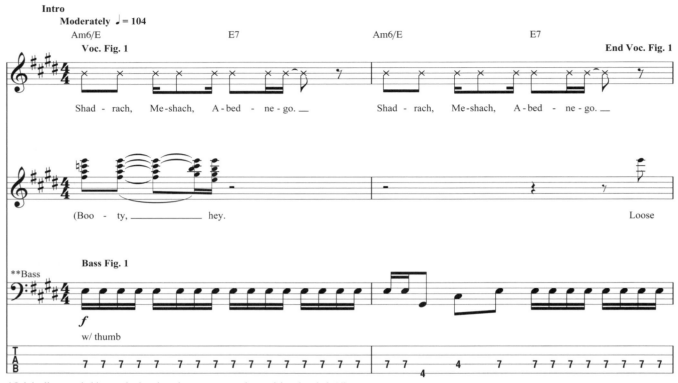

*Originally recorded in standard tuning, the tape was sped up, raising the pitch 1/2 step.
**Rustee Allen

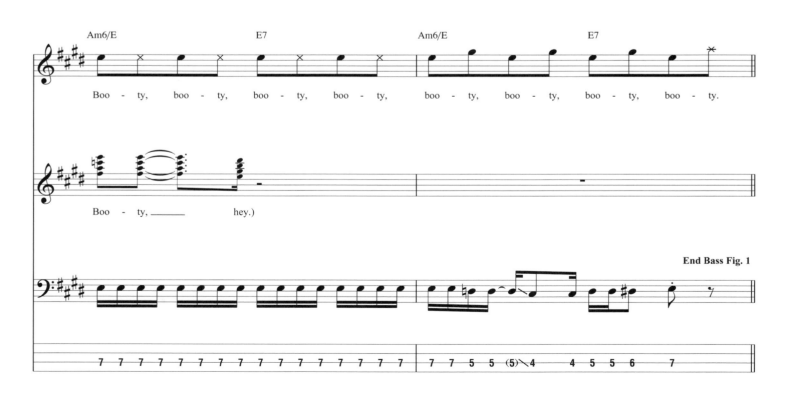

Interlude

Bkgd. Voc.: w/ Voc. Fig. 1 (4 times)

E7

Voc. Fig. 2

A - bed - ne - go. ___   Shad - rach, a - Me -shach,   A - bed - ne - go. ___

Female: (Boo - ty.) ___

Bass Fig. 2

Harm. - - -⌐   Harm. - - - - - - - - - -⌐   w/ thumb & finger⌐

slight P.M. -

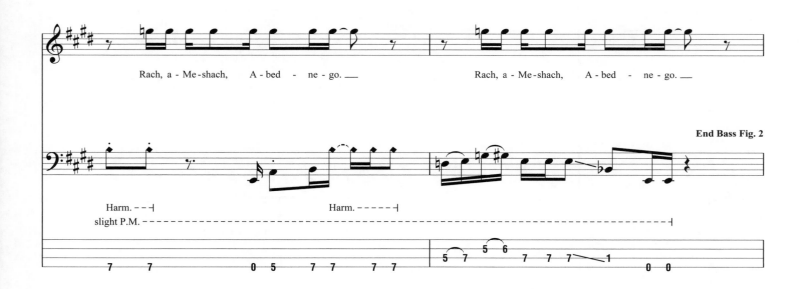

Rach, a - Me -shach,   A - bed - ne - go. ___   Rach, a - Me -shach,   A - bed - ne - go. ___

End Bass Fig. 2

Harm. - - -⌐   Harm. - - - - - -⌐

slight P.M. -⌐

Voc.: w/ Voc. Fig. 2
Bass: w/ Bass Fig. 2

Female: (Boo - ty. ___)   Hey,   hey,

hey, — hey, — hey, — hey, — hey, — yeah.) *Male:* 1. Well, _____

When you're try-in' to flee from, ____ oo, I'll tell you what to do ____ from, ____

(An - y fak - in' grin, ____ in the

ha, ha. ____ Find your - self some roots to ____

frame of mind I'm in. ____

50

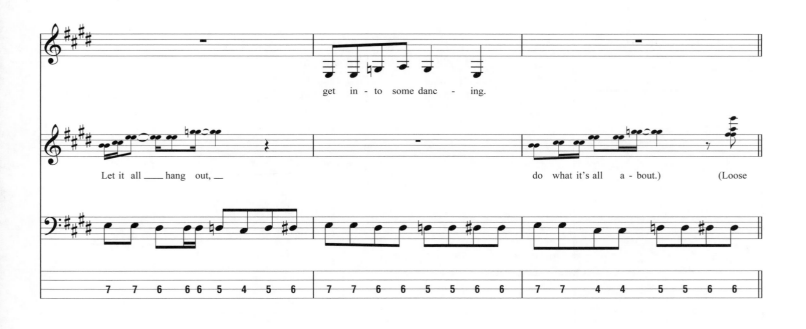

Chorus
Bkgd. Voc.: w/ Voc. Fig. 1 (1 1/2 times)

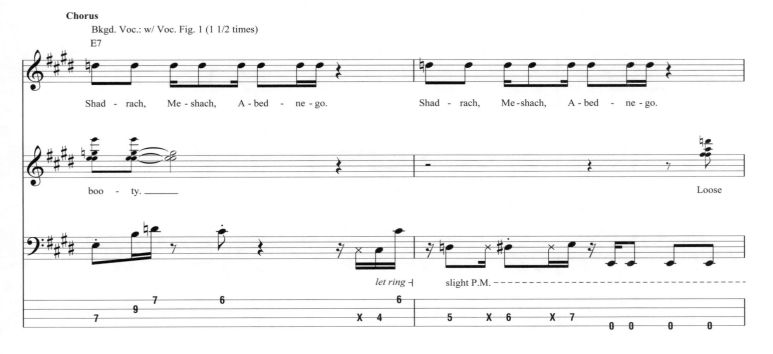

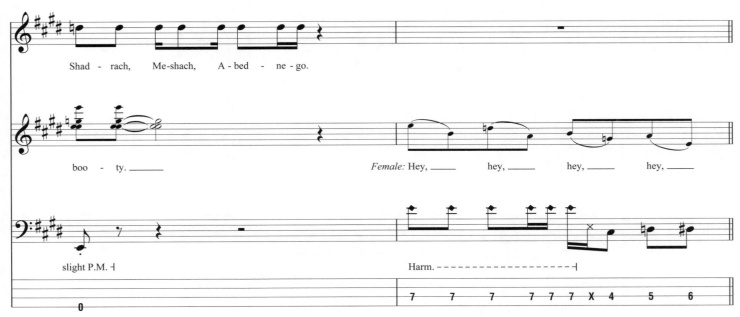

Verse

E7

2. Life can be con - fus - ing, mm, ___ and if ___

hey, ___ hey.) *Male & Female:* (Ev - 'ry giv - en day, ___

___ you feel like los - ing. This stuff will be a - maz - ing, ___

get on out the way. ___

how min - utes turn to days in. ___

Here is all you do, ___ do - in' what I do.) ___ (Loose

Bridge

Bkgd. Voc.: w/ Voc. Fig. 1 (2 1/2 times)

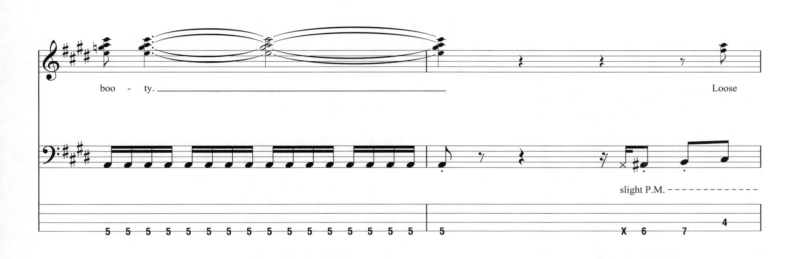

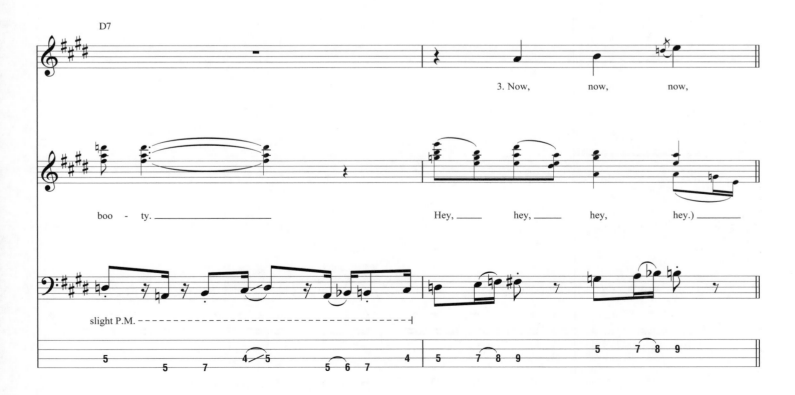

Verse

E7

now I got to get on. ___ Don't

(See you in the mind. ___)

*Harm.

*Touch string at 12th fret w/ fretting finger.

wan - na see you fret on. ___

Leave them blues be - hind. ___

Hold it 'til you're set free. ___

Watch them all ___ be free. ___

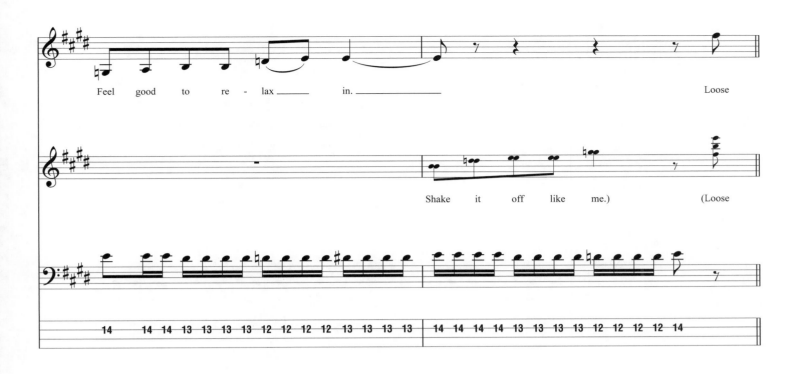

Chorus

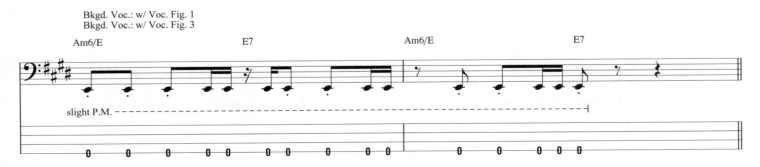

Interlude

Bkgd. Voc.: w/ Voc. Fig. 1
Bkgd. Voc.: w/ Voc. Fig. 3 (1 1/2 times)
Bass: w/ Bass Fig. 1

Boo - ty, boo - ty, boo - ty, boo - ty,   boo - ty, boo - ty, boo - ty, boo - ty.

Outro

Bkgd. Voc.: w/ Voc. Fig. 1 (2 times)
Bass: w/ Bass Fig. 2

A - bed - ne - go. __   Shad - rach, a - Me-shach,   A - bed - ne - go. __

Female: (Boo - ty.) _____

Rach, a - Me-shach,   A - bed - ne - go. __   Rach, a - Me-shach,   A - bed - ne - go. __

Bkgd. Voc.: w/ Voc. Fig. 1 (till fade)
Bass: w/ Bass Fig. 2 (till fade)

A - bed - ne - go. __   Shad - rach, a - Me-shach,   A - bed - ne - go. __

Female: (Boo - ty.) _____

Repeat and fade

Rach, a - Me-shach,   A - bed - ne - go. __   Rach, a - Me-shach,   A - bed - ne - go. __

Sing a Simple Song

Words and Music by Sylvester Stewart

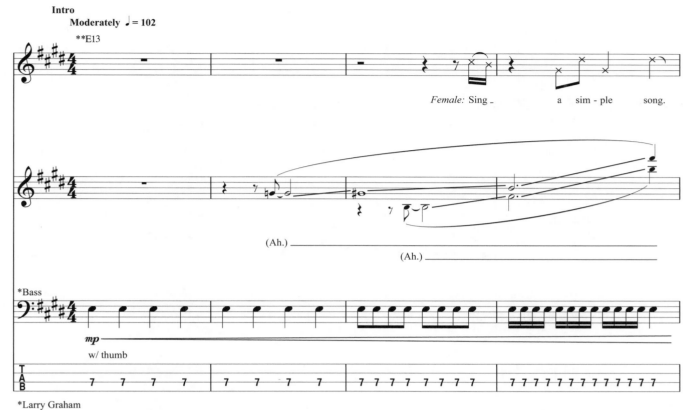

*Larry Graham

**Chord symbols reflect overall harmony.

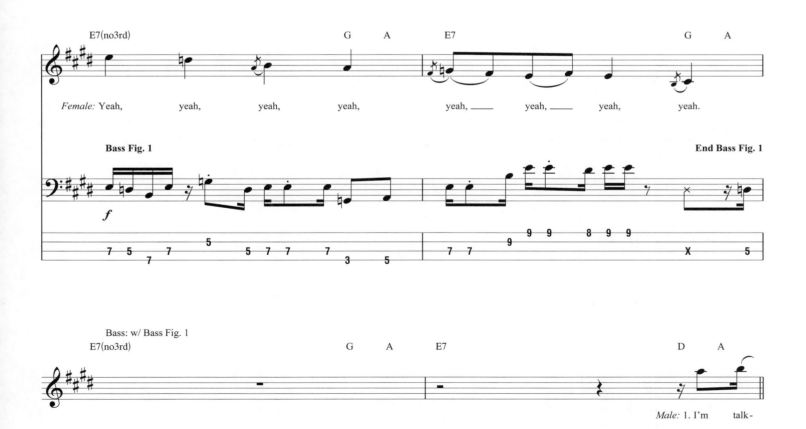

Verse

- in', talk - in', talk - in', talk - in', talk - in' in __ my sleep. _____ I'm walk -

- in', __ walk - in', __ walk - in', walk - in', walk - in' in __ the street, uh! Time _

___ is pass - ing, I __ grow old - er, things __ are hap - 'nin' fast. _____ All _

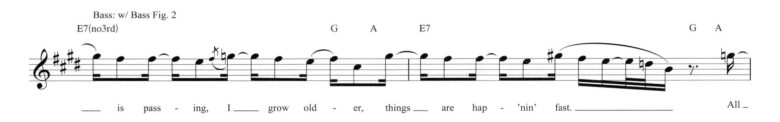

___ I have __ to hold __ on - to ___ is a sim - ple song __ at last. Let me hear you say. _

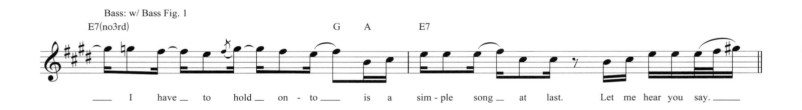

Chorus

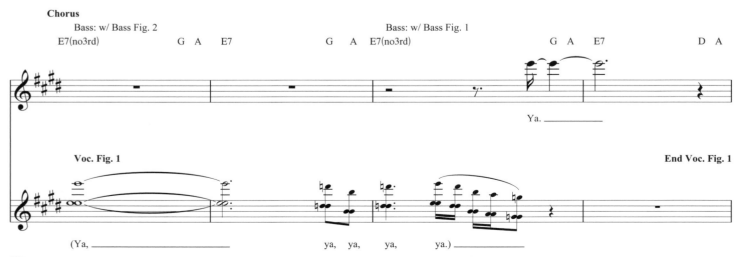

Ya. _____

(Ya, _____ ya, ya, ya, ya.) _____

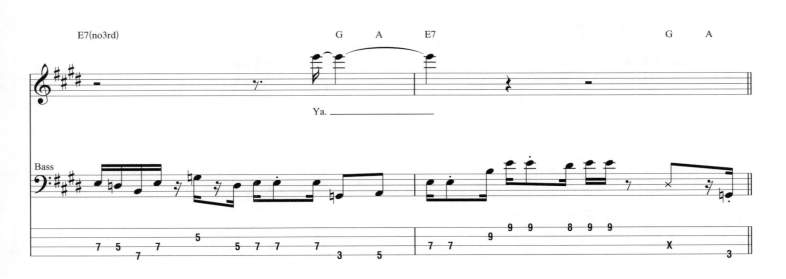

Ya. ____

Bridge

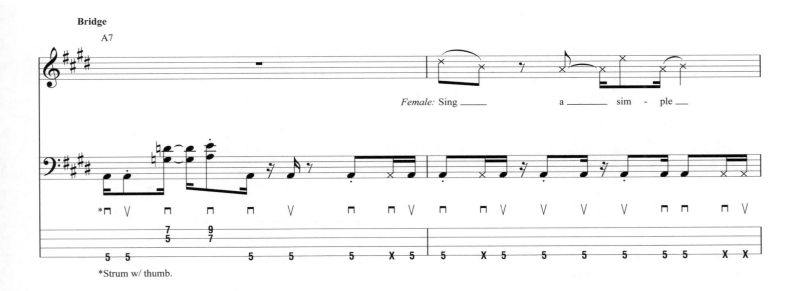

Female: Sing ____ a ____ sim - ple

*Strum w/ thumb.

song.

Try a lit - tle ____

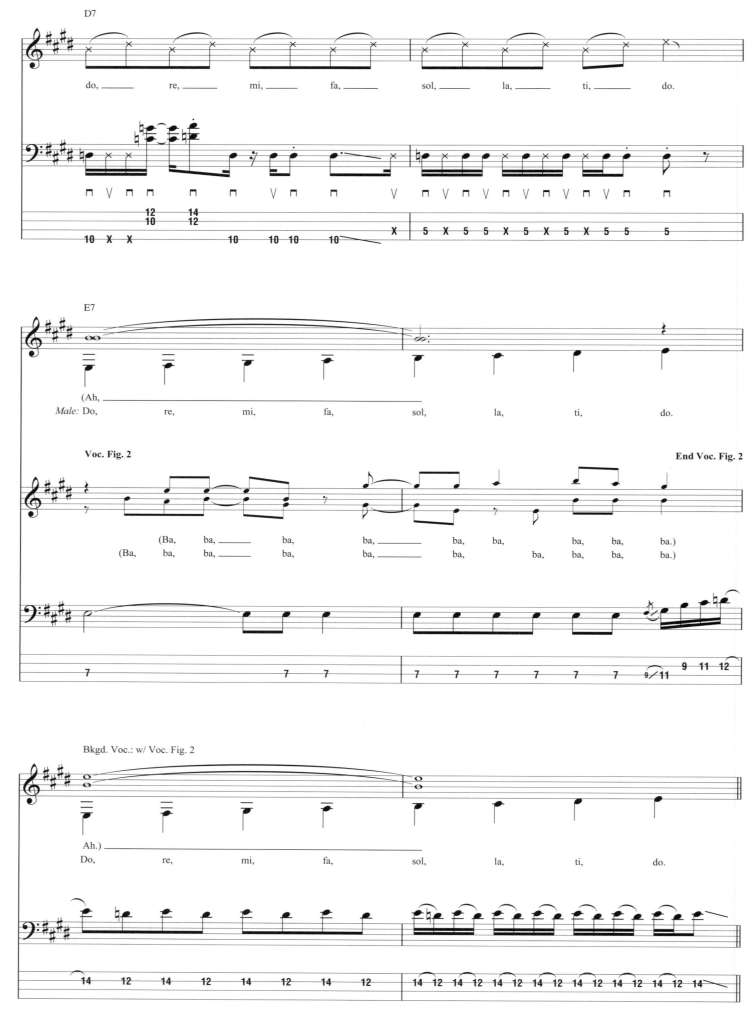

Interlude

Female: Yeah, yeah, yeah, yeah, yeah,— yeah,— yeah, yeah.

Male: 2. I'm liv-

Verse

Bass: w/ Bass Fig. 2 (3 times)

-in', liv-in', liv-in', life _____ with all its ups ___ and downs. _____ I'm giv-

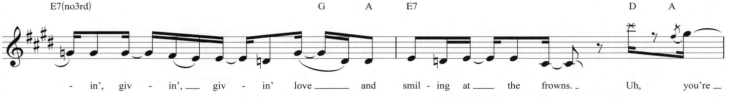

-in', giv-in',— giv-in' love _____ and smil-ing at ___ the frowns. _ Uh, you're _

___ in trou-ble when ___ you find ___ it's hard ___ for you to smile. _____ A

Bass: w/ Bass Fig. 1

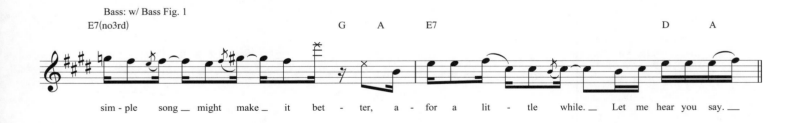

sim-ple song ___ might make ___ it bet-ter, a- for a lit-tle while. __ Let me hear you say.

Chorus

Bkgd. Voc.: w/ Voc. Fig. 1 (2 times)
Bass: w/ Bass Fig. 2

Bass: w/ Bass Fig. 1

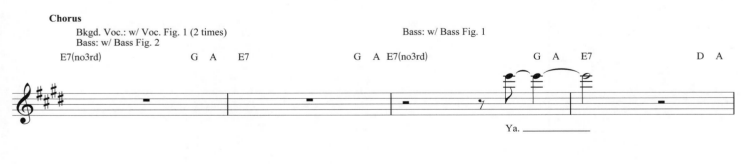

Ya. _____

Bass: w/ Bass Fig. 2

Bass: w/ Bass Fig. 1

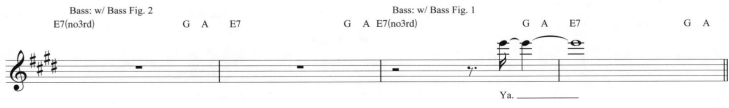

Ya. _____

Interlude

Verse

Outro-Chorus

from *Greatest Hits*

Thank You
(Falletinme Be Mice Elf Again)

Words and Music by Sylvester Stewart

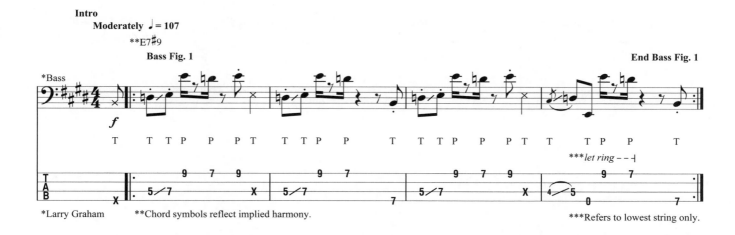

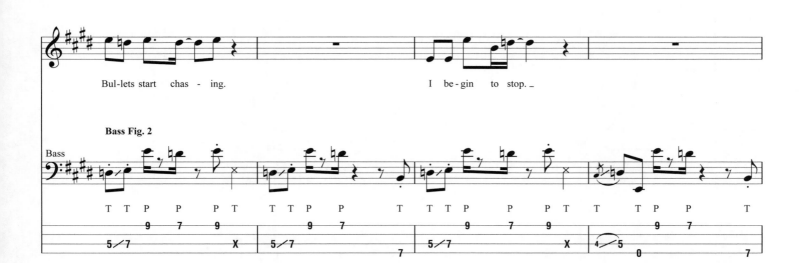

We be-gin to wres - tle.   I was on the top.   I _____ want to

End Bass Fig. 2

T T P P P T T T T P P T T T P P P T T T P P T

*let ring - - - ⌐|

*As before

Chorus

Bass: w/ Bass Fig. 2 (1st 7 meas.)

E7#9

thank you   for let-ting me   be my - self   a - gain. __

Thank you   for let - ting me   be my - self   a - gain. __

Interlude

N.C.(E5)

Bass

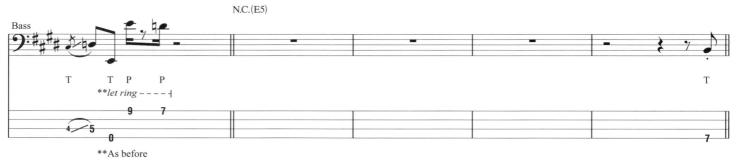

T   T P P   T

**let ring - - - - ⌐|

**As before

𝄋 Verse

Bass: w/ Bass Fig. 2

E7#9

2. Stiff all in the col - lar,   fluff - y in the face. __
3. Dance to the mus - ic,   all night long. __

Chit - chat chat - ter try - in',   s - shtuff - y in the place. __
Ev - 'ry-day peo - ple,   sing a sim - ple song. __

Thank you for the par - ty,
Ma-ma's so ___ hap - py.

but I could nev - er stay. _
Ma - ma start to cry. _

To Coda ⊕

Ma-ny things ___ on ___ my mind; _
Pop - pa's still sing - ing

words in the way. _
you can make it if you try. _

I ___ want to

Chorus
Bass: w/ Bass Fig. 2 (last 4 meas.)

E7#9

thank you for let - ting me by my - self a - gain. _

Bass: w/ Bass Fig. 1

Thank you for let - ting me be my - self a - gain. _

D.S. al Coda

Interlude

Bass tacet

N.C.(E5)

3

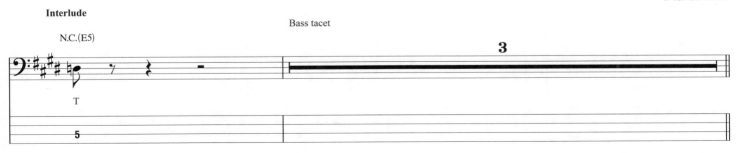

Coda

Chorus
Bass: w/ Bass Fig. 2

E7#9

thank you for let-ting me, oh, yeah, __ be my-self a - gain. __

Diff-'rent strokes for dif-fer-ent folks, yeah, __

Thank you for let-ting me be my-self a - gain. __

_____ yeah.

Verse
Bass: w/ Bass Fig. 1 (2 times)

E7#9

4. Fram-ing eyes __ of peo-ple, fear __ burn-ing in-to you. Ma-ny men __ are miss-ing much, hate what they do. __

Youth and truth __ are mak-ing love. __ Dig it for a start - er. Dy-in' young __ is hard to take; __ sell-in' out is hard - er.

Chorus
Bass: w/ Bass Fig. 2 (2 times)

E7#9

Thank you for let-ting me be my-self a - gain. __ I _____ want to

thank you   for let-ting me   be   my - self   a - gain. __

Thank you   for   let-ting me   be my - self   a -

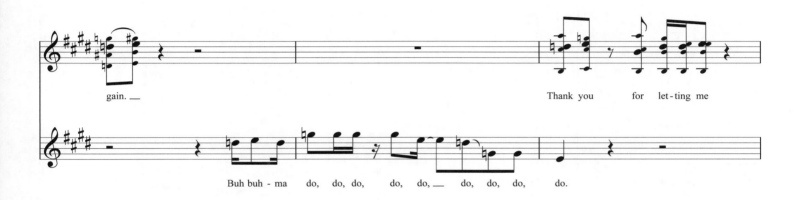

gain. __   Thank you   for let-ting me

Buh buh - ma   do, do, do,   do, do, __ do, do, do,   do.

be my - self   a - gain. __   I _____ want to

Begin fade

Bass: w/ Bass Fig. 2

E7#9

thank you   for let-ting me   be my - self   a - gain. __   I _____ want to

Repeat and fade

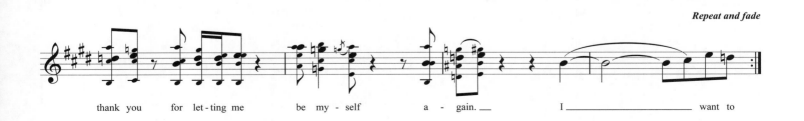

thank you   for let-ting me   be my - self   a - gain. __   I _____ want to

from *There's a Riot Goin' On*

Thank You for Talkin' to Me Africa

Words and Music by Sylvester Stewart

*Larry Graham

**All non-slapped notes are plucked w/ thumb.

***Octaves are played by simultaneously strumming the lower note with the thumb and popping the top note with the index finger.

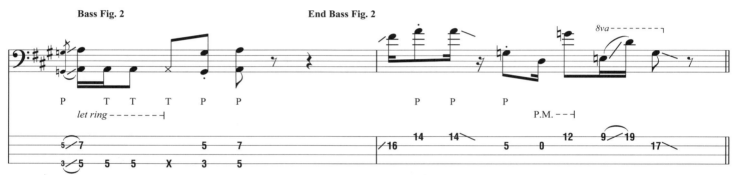

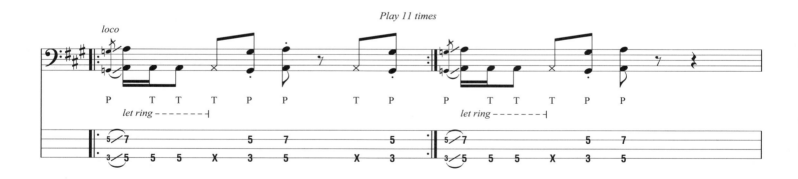

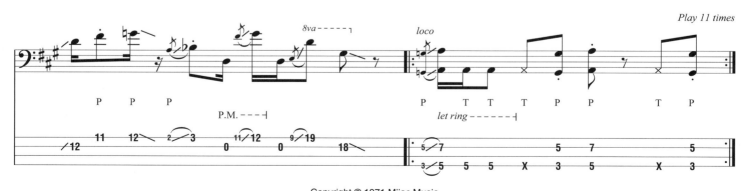

I was on ___ the top. ___ Hey, ___ hey. ___

(I was on the top.) ___

Chorus

Bass: w/ Bass Fig. 1 (6 times)

A9(no3rd)

Thank you. (For ___ let - tin' me be my - self ___ a - gain. ___ Uh, ___ ah.

A7

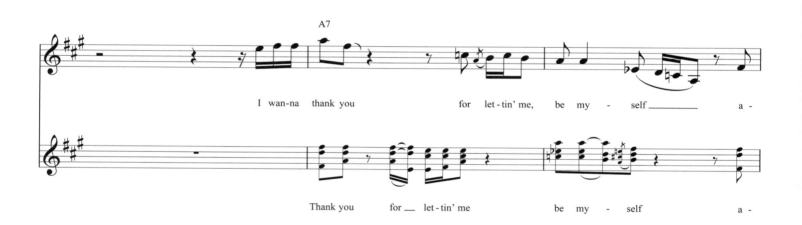

I wan-na thank you for ___ let - tin' me, be my - self ___ a-

Thank you for ___ let - tin' me be my - self a-

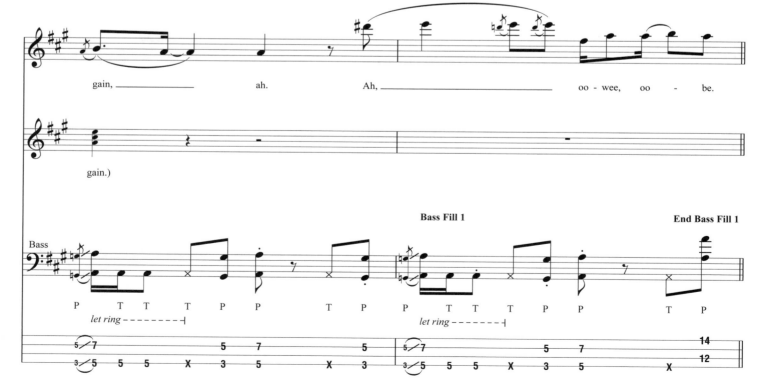

gain, ___ ah. Ah, ___ oo - wee, oo - be.

gain.)

Bass Fill 1　　　　　　　　　　　　　　**End Bass Fill 1**

Bass

P　T　T　T　P　P　T　P　P　T　T　T　P　P　T　P

let ring - - - - - - - ┘　　　　*let ring* - - - - - - - ┘

Verse

A7

Bass Fig. 3

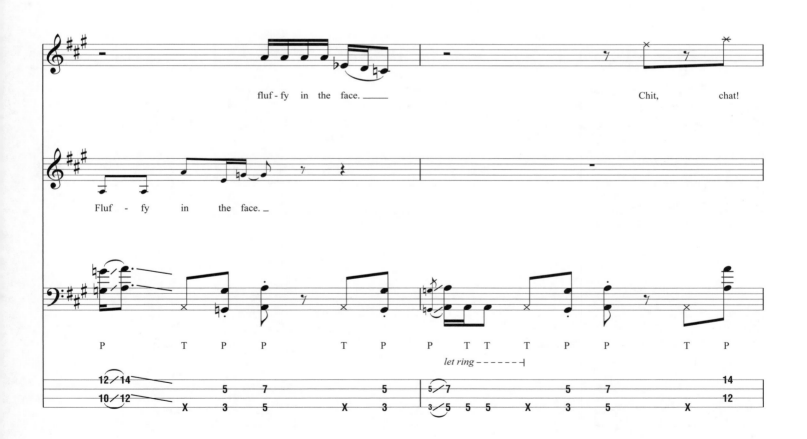

Hey! ___ Yeah, ___ yay. Oh.

Chit - chat, chat - ter try - in'.

P T P P T P P T T T P P T P

let ring - - - - - -

```
14/17                5     7           5   5/7           5     7         14
12/15           X    3     5      X    3   3/5 5  5  5   X    3     5   X  12
```

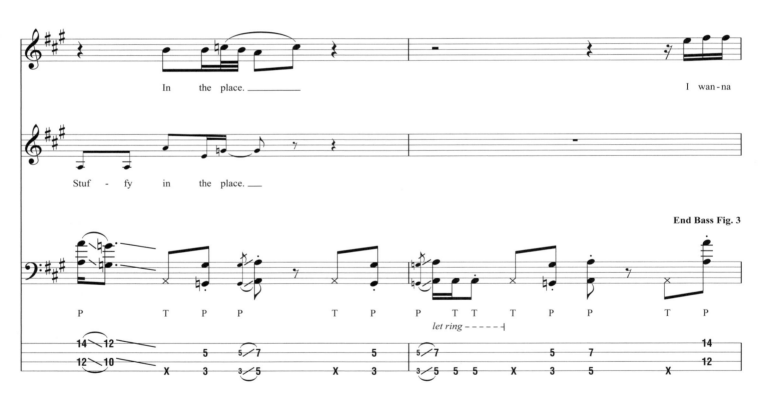

In the place. ___ I wan - na

Stuf - fy in the place. ___

End Bass Fig. 3

P T P P T P P T T T P P T P

let ring - - - - -

```
14\12              5   5/7         5   5/7           5     7         14
12\10           X  3   3/5    X    3  3/5 5 5    X   3     5      X  12
```

Bass: w/ Bass Fig. 1 (7 times)

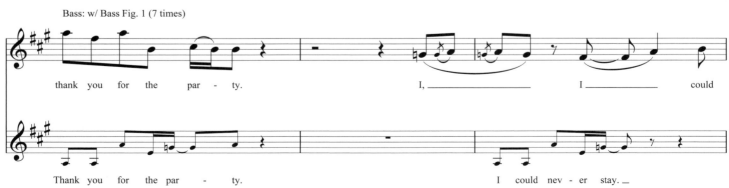

thank you for the par - ty. I, ___ I ___ could

Thank you for the par - ty. I could nev - er stay. ___

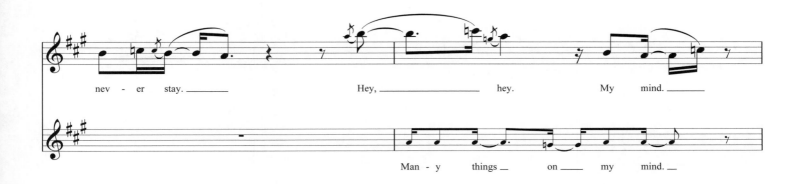

never stay. _____ Hey, _____ hey. My mind. _____

Man - y things _____ on _____ my mind. _____

Bass: w/ Bass Fig. 2

Man - y things on my mind. _____ Hey, _____ oh, _____ oo. _____

Words in the way.)

Chorus

Bass: w/ Bass Fig. 1 (8 times)

A7

Thank you for let - tin' me be my - self _____ a - gain. Whoa, _____

(Thank you for let - tin' me be my - self _____ a - gain. _____

yeah. _____ Yeah, _____

I wan - na thank you for let - tin' me

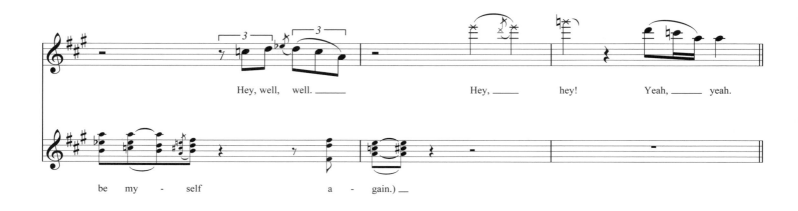

Hey, well, well. _____ Hey, _____ hey! Yeah, _____ yeah.

be my - self a - gain.) _____

Verse

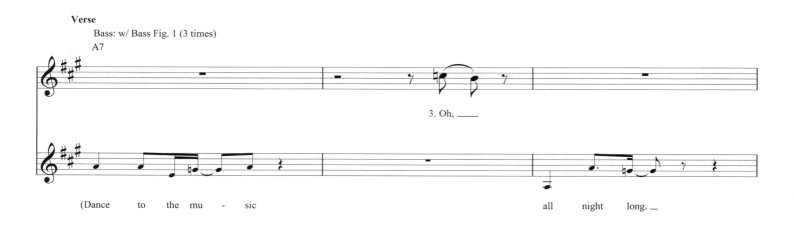

Bass: w/ Bass Fig. 1 (3 times)

A7

3. Oh, _____

(Dance to the mu - sic all night long. _____

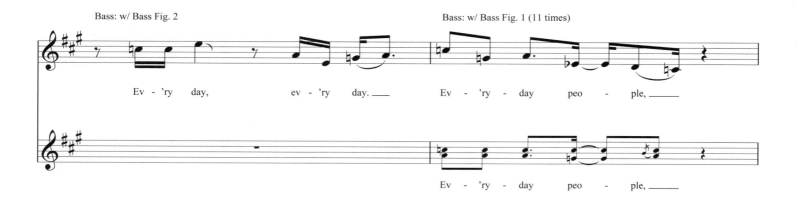

Bass: w/ Bass Fig. 2   Bass: w/ Bass Fig. 1 (11 times)

Ev - 'ry day, ev - 'ry day. _____ Ev - 'ry - day peo - ple, _____

Ev - 'ry - day peo - ple, _____

young child, sing a sim - ple song. A sim - ple, last - ing song, _____

sing a sim - ple song.

well. Ma-ma, Ma-ma's so hap - py, _____ ha, how. _____

Ma-ma's so hap - py.

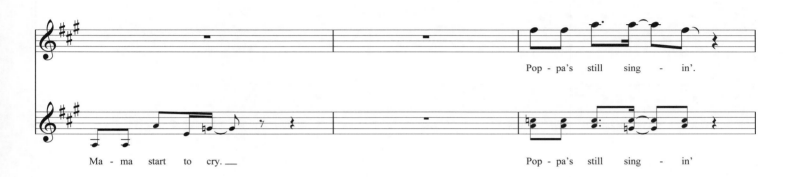

Pop - pa's still sing - in'.

Ma - ma start to cry. ___ Pop - pa's still sing - in'

Bass: w/ Bass Fig. 2

Pop-pa's still sing - in' you can make it, you can make it, make it. Hey. ___

you can make it if you try. ___ Aw. ___

Chorus
Bass: w/ Bass Fig. 1 (8 times)
A7

I've _____ got - ta,

Voc. Fig. 1   **End Voc. Fig. 1**

(Thank you for let -tin' me be my - self a - gain.) ___

Bkgd. Voc.: w/ Voc. Fig. 1

Well, _ Ho! Yeah. Do, do, ___ do, do, ___ yeah, yeah. ___

You Can Make It if You Try

Words and Music by Sylvester Stewart

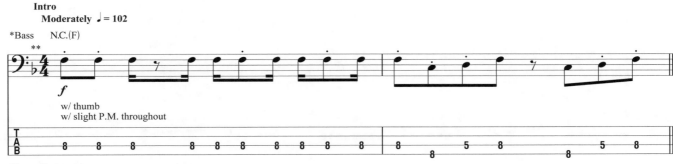

*Larry Graham

**Originally recorded in F, the tape was sped up, raising the pitch approx. 1/4 step.

Verse

F7

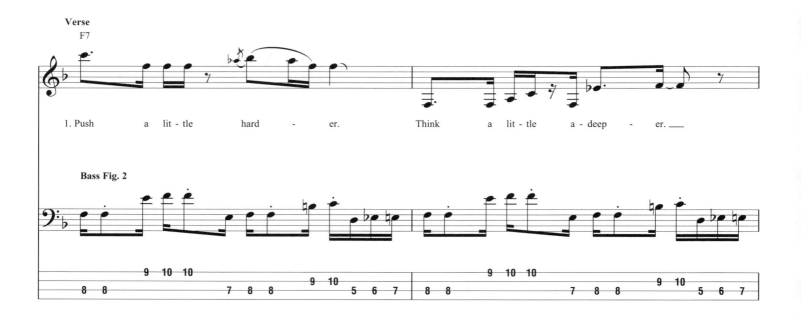

1. Push a lit - tle hard - er. Think a lit - tle a - deep - er. ___

Bass Fig. 2

Don't let the plas - tic bring you down. ___ *Female:* All to - geth - er now!

End Bass Fig. 2

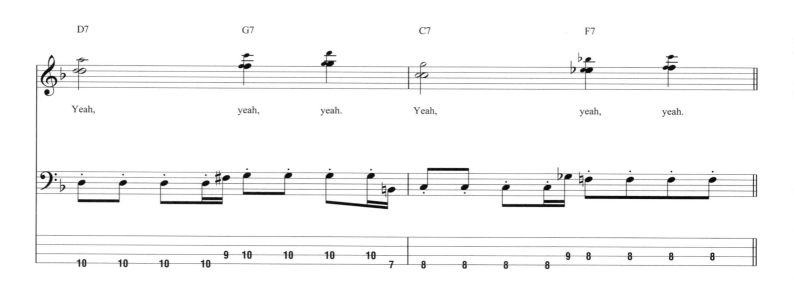

D7   G7   C7   F7

Yeah, yeah, yeah. Yeah, yeah, yeah.

Interlude

D.S. al Coda

Coda

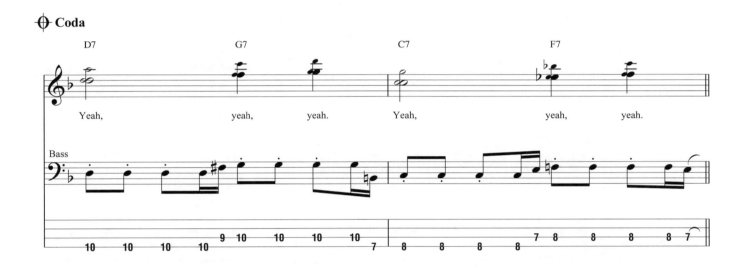

Yeah,   yeah,   yeah.   Yeah,   yeah,   yeah.

Chorus

You   can — make   it.   Ma,   ma - ma - ma - ma - ma - ma - ma - ma,

(You   can   make   it   if   you   try. ———

w/ thumb & index finger

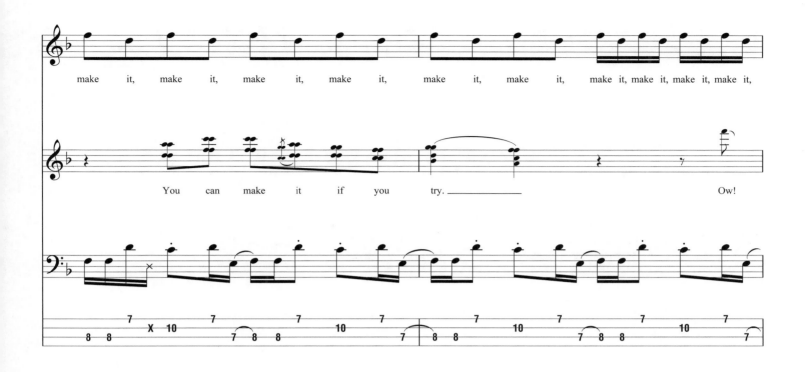

make it, make it, make it, make it, make it, make it, make it, make it, make it, make it,

You can make it if you try. _____ Ow!

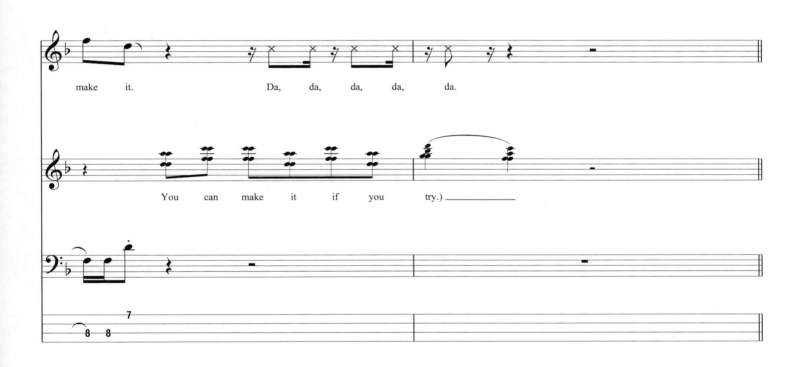

make it. Da, da, da, da, da.

You can make it if you try.) _____

Interlude

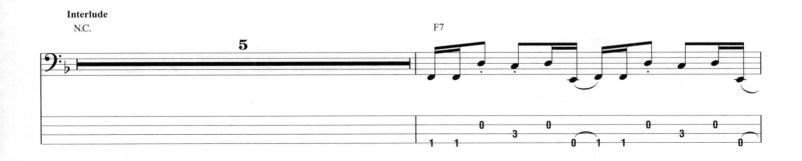

N.C.

F7

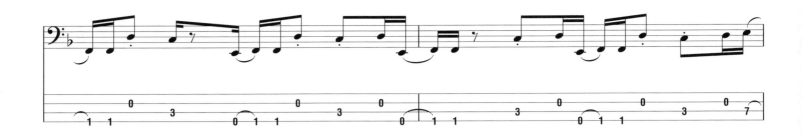

F9

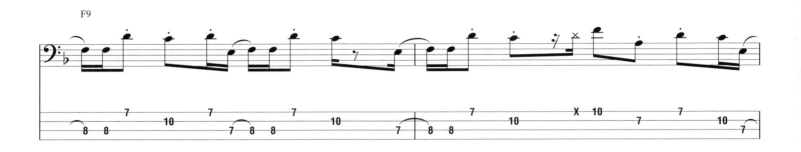

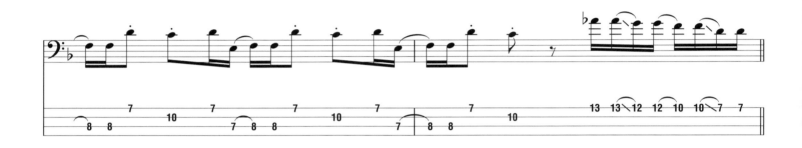

Chorus

F9

Uh, you can

(You can make it if you try. _____ Oh! _____)

make it, make it, make it, make it. Make it ma - ma, make it ma - ma, make it ma - ma, make it ma - ma,

make it. You can

Fade out

make it.

from *There's a Riot Goin' On*

(You Caught Me) Smilin'

Words and Music by Sylvester Stewart

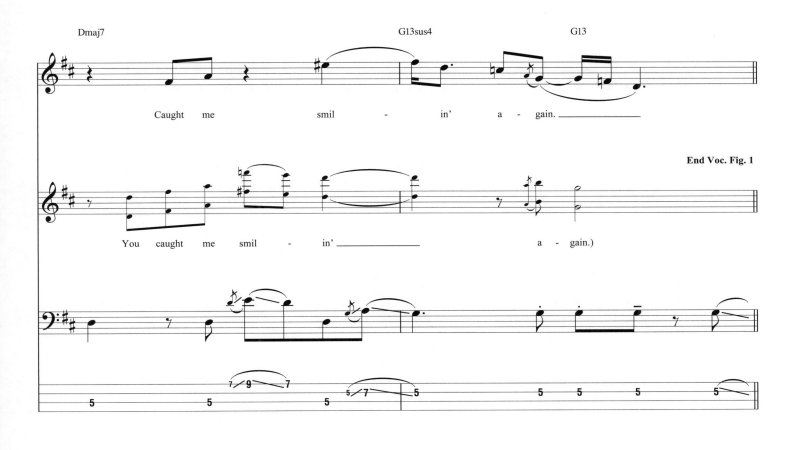

Caught me smil - in' a - gain.

End Voc. Fig. 1

You caught me smil - in' a - gain.)

Verse

2. I'll ___ be gone, ___ it won't take you ___ long to ___

___ climb a ___ tree a - bout ___ me. ___

Interlude

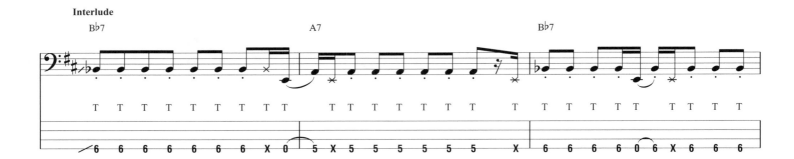

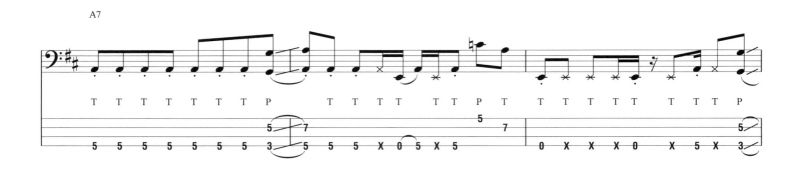

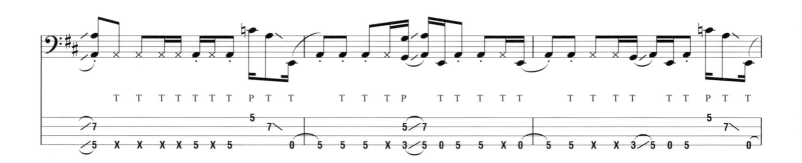

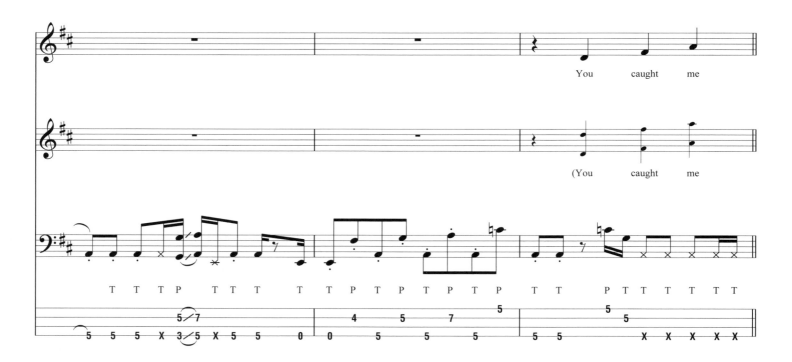

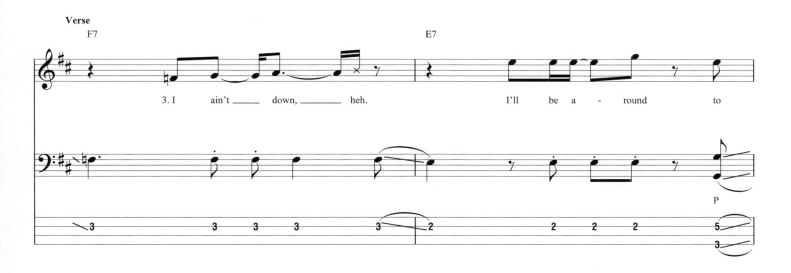

Chorus

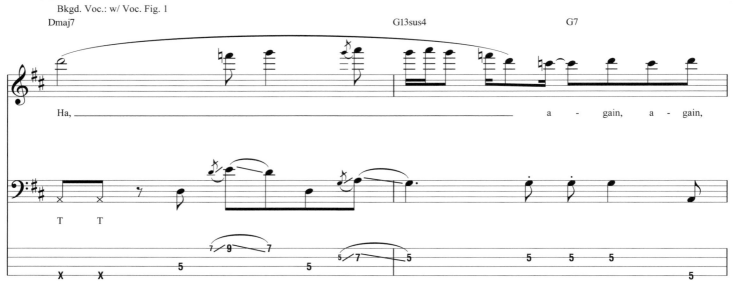

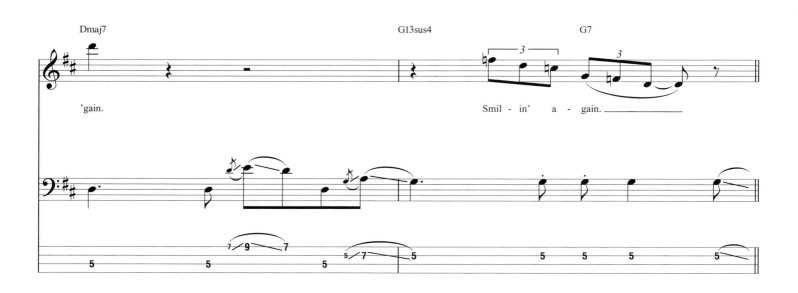

Verse

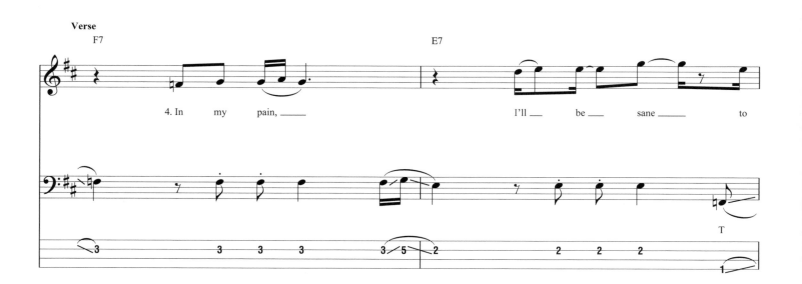

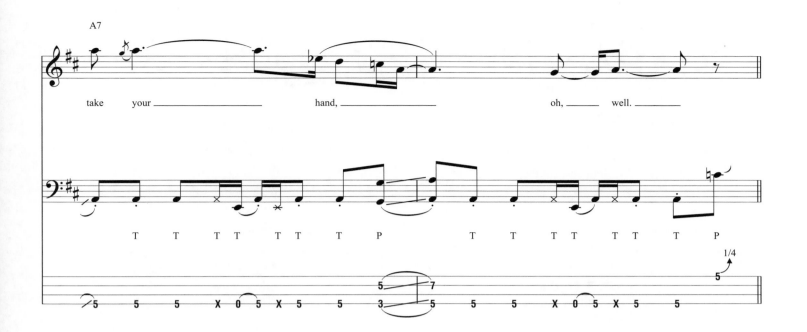

take your _____ hand, _____ oh, _____ well. _____

Interlude

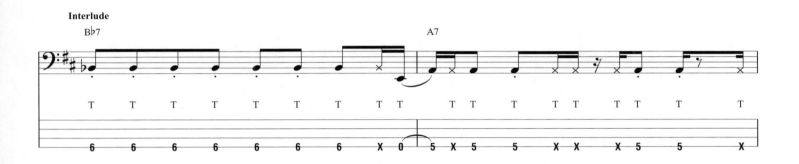

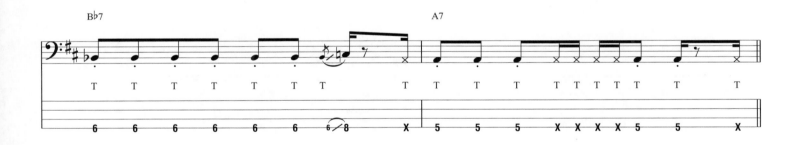

Outro

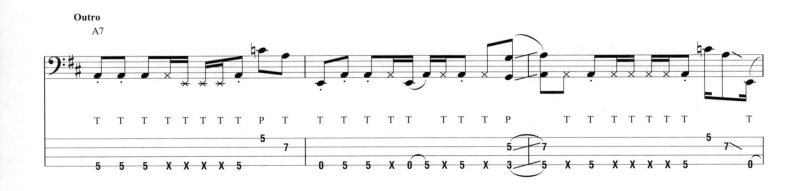

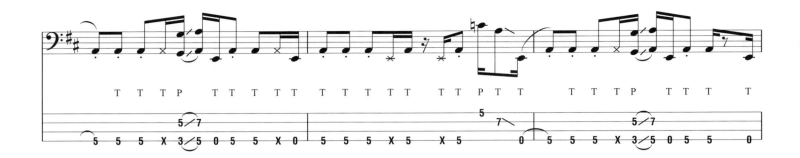

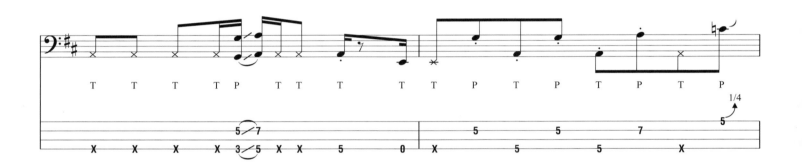

Begin fade

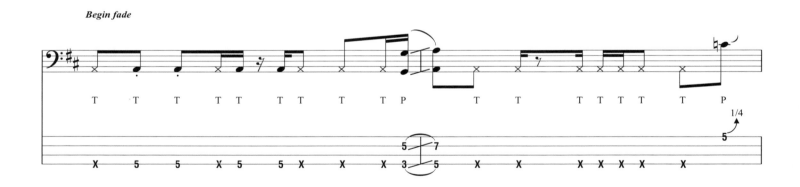

Fade out

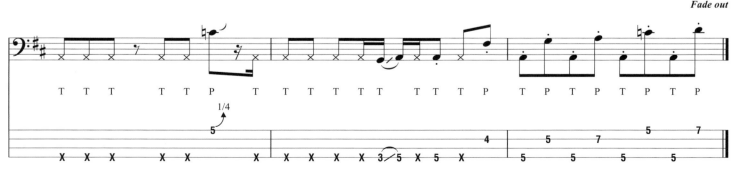